JUL   2009

BENJAMIN FRANKLIN

The Man Who Could Do
Just about Anything

AMERICAN HEROES

BENJAMIN FRANKLIN

*The Man Who Could Do
Just about Anything*

SNEED B. COLLARD III

Marshall Cavendish
Benchmark
New York

For my electric editor, Joyce Stanton,
a friend and favorite Franklin-o-phile.

Marshall Cavendish Benchmark
99 White Plains Road
Tarrytown, New York 10591-9001
www.marshallcavendish.us

Library of Congress Cataloging-in-Publication Data
Collard, Sneed B.
Benjamin Franklin : the man who could do just about anything / by Sneed B. Collard III.
p. cm. — (American heroes)
Summary: "A juvenile biography of Benjamin Franklin, scientist, inventor, printer, writer, statesman,
and Founding Father" —Provided by publisher.
Includes index.
ISBN-13: 978-0-7614-2161-0
ISBN-10: 0-7614-2161-0
1. Franklin, Benjamin, 1706–1790—Juvenile literature. 2. Statesmen—United States—Biography—
Juvenile literature. 3. Inventors—United States—Biography—Juvenile literature. 4. Scientists—United States—
Biography—Juvenile literature. 5. Printers—United States—Biography—Juvenile literature.
I. Title II. Series: Collard, Sneed B. American heroes.

E302.6.F8C678 2006
973.3092—dc22   2005027942

Editor: Joyce Stanton
Editorial Director: Michelle Bisson
Art Director: Anahid Hamparian
Series Designer and Compositor: Anne Scatto / PIXEL PRESS
Printed in Malaysia
3 5 6 4 2

Images provided by Rose Corbett Gordon, Art Editor, Mystic CT, from the following sources:
Front cover: Stock Montage/Getty Images
Back cover: The Granger Collection, New York
Page i: Stock Montage/Getty Images; *pages ii, 8,11, 15, 23, 24:* The Granger Collection, New York; *page vi:* The Corcoran Gallery of Art/Corbis; *pages 1, 3, 4, 28:* The Art Archive/Culver Pictures; *page 7:* Giraudon/Art Resource, NY; *page 12:* Private Collection/Lawrence Steigrad Fine Arts, New York/Bridgeman Art Library; *page 16:* Bettmann/Corbis; *page 19:* Stock Montage/SuperStock; *page 20:* Guildhall Art Gallery, London/HIP/Art Resource, NY; *pages 27, 34:* Réunion des Musées Nationaux/Art Resource, NY; *page 31:* Art Resource, NY; *page 32:* North Wind Picture Archives.

CONTENTS

Benjamin Franklin
1

Important Dates
34

Words to Know
35

To Learn More about Ben Franklin
37

Index
39

The time Ben spent playing outdoors gave him a fascination with nature.

B Franklin

As a boy, Benjamin Franklin was always curious. One day he was flying his kite when he got an idea. He wondered if his kite could pull him through water so he wouldn't have to swim. To find out, Ben took off his clothes. He waded into a pond. He held the kite string in his hands and floated on his back. To his delight, the kite pulled him all the way across the pond.

Ben Franklin's curiosity would last his entire lifetime. It helped him become a great scientist and inventor. But Ben was much more. During his long life, he became one of America's most important writers, thinkers, and leaders.

Benjamin Franklin was the twelfth of seventeen children. He was born in Boston, Massachusetts, on January 17, 1706. Today, Massachusetts is a part of the United States. But when Ben was born, Massachusetts was a colony of Great Britain.

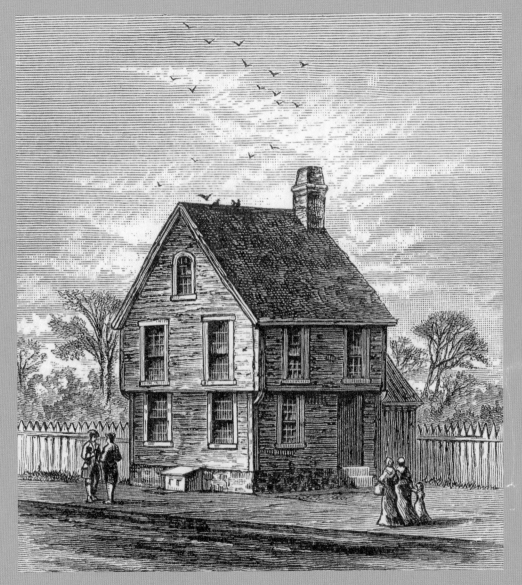

Ben was born in this house in Boston, Massachusetts,
on January 17, 1706.

When he was only twelve, Ben began to work in his brother's print shop.

Ben's father was a candle and soap maker. He believed in hard work, but not schooling. Ben spent only two years in a classroom. Then, when Ben was twelve, his father sent him to learn a trade. Ben became an apprentice to his older brother James.

James was a printer and, at first, Ben enjoyed the work. In the print shop, he eagerly read the many books and newspapers around him. They helped feed his curiosity about the world.

In 1721, James started his own newspaper. Ben began writing for it. Under false names such as Silence Dogwood, Ben wrote funny letters and essays. His writing poked fun at powerful people in Boston. It also urged fairness and freedom. He wrote, "Without freedom of thought there can be no such thing as wisdom." And without freedom of speech, he told people, there can be no such thing as liberty.

People in Boston enjoyed reading Ben's funny letters and interesting essays.

His brother's temper helped drive Ben away from Boston.

Ben had a desire to be free himself. He had learned many things as an apprentice, but his brother James did not give him the respect he wanted. When he was angry, James even beat Ben. By the time he was seventeen years old, Ben had had enough. He left his brother's print shop and ran away to Philadelphia, Pennsylvania. There he found work with other printers. Afterward, he spent a year in London, the capital of Great Britain. When he returned, Ben started his own print shop and newspaper. He was now twenty-two years old. His star was rising fast.

Ben worked hard and became one of the most successful printers in Philadelphia. He got married and raised a family. At the same time, Ben worked to improve life for others. He helped start one of America's first libraries. He organized Philadelphia's first official fire department. He also helped build a meeting hall where people from any religion could speak. When France threatened to invade Pennsylvania, Ben helped organize men to fight.

Ben and his wife, Deborah Read, had three children, two boys and a girl.
One of the boys, William, became governor of New Jersey.

Poor Richard's Almanack *served as a guide for living,
and a way for Ben to express his own beliefs.*

All this time, Ben shaped his own rules for living. Every year, he published a book called *Poor Richard's Almanack*. These books contained many witty sayings to help people live good lives:

- Eat to live, and not live to eat.
- A good example is the best sermon.
- The sleeping fox catches no poultry.
- No gains without pain.
- God helps them that help themselves.

Ben borrowed most of the sayings from other people, but they reflected ideas that Ben himself tried to follow.

By 1748, Ben had made enough money to retire. At the age of forty-two, he decided to let a partner run his printing and newspaper business. Ben devoted the next few years to science and invention. He made discoveries about weather. He designed better stoves. One day he remembered a visit he had made to a traveling science show. The showman did tricks with electricity. Ben was fascinated.

At this time, people understood very little about electricity. Ben began to change that. Using glass tubes, he experimented with electric charge and current.

*Using glass tubes, Ben performed experiments
with electricity.*

*With the help of a kite, Ben discovered that lightning
and electricity were the same thing.*

Ben discovered that electricity has two charges, positive and negative. He also invented the first battery. Then, he began thinking about lightning.

For years, scientists had wondered if lightning and electricity were the same thing. No one knew, but Ben decided to find out. He designed several experiments. In one, he used a kite to try to pull electricity from a storm cloud. It worked! Using this information, Ben began setting up metal rods to attract lightning safely away from houses. "Lightning rods" still protect buildings around the world today.

By now, Benjamin Franklin had become a successful writer, businessman, and scientist. He still had one important role to play—leader.

Since the time of the Pilgrims, the American colonies had been ruled by Great Britain. But by the mid-1700s many colonists, including Ben, believed that Britain was treating them unfairly. Great Britain, for example, could tax colonists without their having any say in the matter.

*By the 1750s, Ben's devotion to business and science
gave way to a passion for politics.*

In London Ben tried to improve relations between Great Britain and the American colonies. But his mission failed.

In his newspaper, Ben began attacking Great Britain's unfair policies. He also began serving in Pennsylvania's colonial government.

In 1757, Ben sailed to London to try to improve relations between the American colonies and Great Britain. His efforts failed. Great Britain refused to treat the colonists fairly, and Ben returned to Philadelphia.

The relationship between the American colonies and Great Britain grew worse. Many Americans now wanted to break away from Britain. At first, Ben didn't want to. He thought Great Britain and America were stronger together than apart. He tried many times to make peace. He even made another voyage across the Atlantic Ocean to try to work things out. It was no use, and Ben once again sailed home.

Despite Ben's efforts, the rulers of Great Britain refused to treat American colonists fairly.

*During the Revolutionary War, Ben helped Thomas Jefferson
write the Declaration of Independence.*

When the Revolutionary War started, Ben's country needed him more than ever. Ben designed fortifications to protect American cities from the British army. He helped organize America's own postal service and became our first postmaster. Even more important, he helped Thomas Jefferson write the Declaration of Independence. This document declared that Americans were free from British rule.

But the colonists couldn't just say they were free. First, they had to win the war with Great Britain, and they needed help.

So, in 1776, at age seventy, Benjamin Franklin left on a top secret mission to France. Ben's mission was to get money and troops from France. Ben's easy, patient manner won over the French. The fighting would last several more years, but France helped America win.

In 1782, Ben Franklin helped work out a formal peace treaty with Great Britain. When it was signed the next year, the United States was finally a free, independent nation.

Ben was a great favorite among the people in France.
His popularity helped him win support for the American cause.

By the time he returned from Europe, Ben was the world's most famous American.

Ben spent almost three more years in Europe. He continued to work on behalf of the United States. He wrote on many subjects and even picked up his scientific studies. Finally, at age seventy-nine, Benjamin Franklin sailed home for the last time. By now, he had become the world's most famous American. The people of Philadelphia cheered for him. They fired cannons in his honor.

Amazingly, Ben's work was not finished. He again served in Pennsylvania's government. He helped make up a new list of rules for living. This list would become our nation's Constitution—the basic laws that govern our country today.

One of Ben's last services to America was to help write our nation's Constitution.

Ben stayed fascinated with the world until he died.

During his final years, Ben continued to invent and to write. Kidney stones and gout often kept him in bed, but he rarely complained. He once wrote, "Upon the whole, I . . . like the world as I find it." When he died on April 19, 1790, he was probably just as curious and pleased as ever. There's no doubt he would be happy to do it all over again.

IMPORTANT DATES

1706 Born on January 17 in Boston, Massachusetts.

1716 Begins working in his father's candle shop.

1718 Works as an apprentice to his brother James.

1723 Runs away to Philadelphia.

1728 Opens his own print shop in Philadelphia.

1730 Marries Deborah Read.

1732 Begins publishing *Poor Richard's Almanack.*

1748 Retires from the printing business.

1752 Conducts experiment pulling electricity from a cloud using a kite.

1757 Travels to London to try to smooth British relations with the colonies.

1764 Again travels to London to try to make peace.

1775 Returns to America to prepare for the War of Independence.

1776 Helps write the Declaration of Independence.

Travels to France to get help to fight the British.

1782 Helps negotiate peace with Great Britain.

1787 Helps write the American Constitution.

1790 Dies on April 17 at age eighty-four.

Words to Know

apprentice Someone who agrees to work for someone else in exchange for training in a trade or skill.

colonist A person who lives in a colony.

colony A territory that is ruled by another country. Colonies are often far away from the country that governs them.

Constitution The document that lists the basic rules for how the government of the United States should be run.

Declaration of Independence The famous document that declared that the American colonies were free from British rule.

essay A piece of writing that expresses opinions and ideas.

fortifications Walls or other structures built to defend against an enemy.

gout A painful disease that causes swelling around a person's joints.

inventor A person who plans and creates new things.

lightning rod A metal rod connected to a building that guides lightning safely into the ground.

postmaster A person in charge of mail services.

Revolutionary War (also known as the American War of Independence) The war that the American colonies fought to win freedom from Great Britain. It lasted from 1775 to 1783.

scientist A person who learns about the world through observations and experiments.

tax To require people to pay money to a government.

treaty An agreement made between two or more nations to cooperate and make peace.

TO LEARN MORE ABOUT BEN FRANKLIN

WEB SITES

Benjamin Franklin: An Extraordinary Life. An Electric Mind.
  www.pbs.org/benfranklin

Ben's Guide to U.S. Government for Kids
  http://bensguide.gpo.gov/benfranklin

The Electric Ben Franklin
  www.ushistory.org/franklin

The Franklin Institute Online
  http://sln.fi.edu/franklin/

The Friends of Franklin, Inc.
  www.benfranklin2006.org

BOOKS

Benjamin Franklin by Ingri and Edgar Parin d'Aulaire, Doubleday
  Books for Young Readers, 1985.

How Ben Franklin Stole the Lightning by Rosalyn Schanzer.
HarperCollins, 2003.

A Picture Book of Benjamin Franklin by David A. Adler. Holiday
House, 1990.

The Remarkable Benjamin Franklin by Cheryl Harness. National
Geographic Children's Books, 2005.

PLACES TO VISIT

The Franklin Institute Science Museum
222 North 20th Street
Philadelphia, Pennsylvania 19103
PHONE: (215) 448-1200 WEB SITE: http://sln.fi.edu/franklin

Smithsonian National Museum of American History
On the National Mall
14th Street and Constitution Avenue, NW
Washington, DC 20560
PHONE: (202) 633-1000 WEB SITE: http://americanhistory.si.edu

INDEX

Page numbers for illustrations are in boldface

American colonies, Great Britain
        and, 2, 18, **20**, 21–22, **23**,
        25, 26

battery, first, 17
Boston, Massachusetts, 2, **3**, 6

Constitution, U.S., 30, **31**

Declaration of Independence,
        24, 25

electricity, 14, **15**, **16**, 17

France, 10, 26, **27**
Franklin, Benjamin, **8**, **11**, **12**,
        32
    books, **12**, 13
    boyhood home, 2, **3**
    childhood and early years,
        vi, 1–2, **4**
    final years, 33

important dates, 34
inventions/scientific studies,
        14, **15**, **16**, 17, 29, 33
leaves Boston, 9
marriage and children, 10, **11**
organizational skills, 10
in Philadelphia, 9
in politics, 18, **19**, 21–22,
        23, **24**, 25–26, **27**,
        29–30, **31**
printing apprenticeship, 5–6,
        9
starts own print
        shop/newspaper, 9–10
Franklin, Deborah (wife), **11**
Franklin, James (brother), **4**, 5, 6,
        8, 9

Great Britain, 2, 9, 18, **20**,
        21–22, **23**, 25, 26

Jefferson, Thomas, **24**, 25

kite, 1, **16**, 17

libraries, America's first, 10
lightning, **16**, 17
lightning rods, 17

Pennsylvania, government, 21, 30
Philadelphia, Pennsylvania, 9,
    21, 29
   first fire department, 10
   meeting hall, 10
Poor Richard's Almanack, **12**, 13

postmaster, first, 25
print shop, **4**
   Ben starts own newspaper
    and, 9–10
   Ben's apprenticeship, 5–6, 9

Revolutionary War, **24**, 25–26

taxes, 18

weather discoveries, 14, **16**

About the Author

SNEED B. COLLARD III is the author of more than fifty award-winning books for young people, including *The Prairie Builders*; *A Platypus, Probably*; *One Night in the Coral Sea*; and the four-book SCIENCE ADVENTURES series for Marshall Cavendish Benchmark. In addition to his writing, Sneed is a popular speaker and presents widely to students, teachers, and the general public. In 2006, he was selected as the Washington Post–Children's Book Guild Nonfiction Award winner for his achievements in children's writing. He is also the author of several novels for young adults, including *Dog Sense* and *Fire Birds*. To learn more about Sneed, visit his Web site at www.sneedbcollardiii.com.